THE FIVE (5) STEPS OF MOVING ON

The most comprehensive book of moving on from heartbreak.

By: Paul Marvin Lumen

Dedication

This book is dedicated to my current daughter Quinn Alpha and all my sons and daughters in the future after I finished writing this book. I believe that time will come, she will fall in love and will get into a relationship. Eventually, in every relationship, there will be always heartaches and disappointments. Before you will find your soulmate, you will eventually face some heartaches and despairs in a relationship. However, it's okay that makes us humans.

So, I write this book so that my children and other people out there who don't know what to do when facing such hurtful situations will cope up with their situations of broken-heartedness through this book. I know this book will be very helpful to them and it will serve as a guide to them on what to do after hurtful and heartache break-ups.

Thank You Message

First, I wanted to thank you to those people who get a copy of this book. I hope through this book I can help you in some ways to recover yourself from distress and sorrows caused by the break-ups. In addition to that, give thanks to yourself because it shows that you want to change or to improve the current state of your relationship.

Introduction

Once again, thank you for showing interest in this book. I believe this book will help you to understand your current relationship status and it will able to guide you steps by steps or ways to move on from your heartbreak.

Heartbreak is very painful to those people who are really in love with their boyfriend/girlfriend especially to the young ones who don't know how to cope up with it. That's why this book was designed to guide for the young ones or even adults who don't know how to handle any break-ups from their relationship. Moreover, some people committed suicide because of break-ups. They don't know how to handle their feelings because they will be trying to suppress and hide their feelings. However, the more you suppress your feelings, the more it gets hurts and it will cause depressions and even suicides.

Before we continue, let me start by introducing myself and how I came up with these steps or ways or guidance or whatever you call it to move on. I am Paul Marvin Lumen, a software engineer, licensed financial advisor, aspiring life/relationship coach, and author. It started when I got into a relationship way back 2009, I was 19 years old at that time. She was my first girlfriend at that time, however, our relationship got ended after I graduated from college, which was three (3) years in a relationship. Our relationship got ended because I found out that she was cheated on me. It was hurtful at first but I told myself at that time that I'm still young and my workplace at that time has lots of beautiful girls. So, I moved on, I started dated other girls, some of them were just one-night-stand, some of them were just friends with benefits and some were just a short time relationship. Until then, I found the girl who had changed me into a better version of myself (that I was I thought so).

The Five (5) Steps of Moving On

In December 2013, I was trying to court a girl and wanted into a serious relationship again. This time, I told myself "I will change myself if this girl will be mine", so after showed my interest and courted her, I got her. As I'd promised to myself, that relationship changed me into a better version of myself. In a way that I became more responsible, faithful and loyal to her and to our dreams. We have conquered it all. I had a lot of plans in the future. So, I decided to put her in to school with my expenses. I paid her tuition, allowances and any projects that she had on her school. I sacrificed my time, energy, and money just to support her and trying to manifest our dreams together.

However, even how perfect our plans and intentions to our relationships, there were some difficulties and hardships that consumed you and only you can do was to let go. After three (3) years in our relationship, she changed and became cold. And she decided to broke up with me for the reasons that I became overprotective to her. She said she wasn't able to enjoy her life because of me. Even how many times I cried and sobbed in front of her and even begging her to stay, nothing changed to her decision.

Consequently, I got nothing to do, I cried nights after nights and even my work got affected because of that broke-up. I blamed myself for what happened to our relationship, I blamed myself that if I wasn't being too overprotective to her, maybe our relationship was still okay and happy. However, after three (3) months from our broke-up, she dated another man and got into the relationship again while I am still trying to get over her that time. So, it was triggered by my confusion and doubts about what she said when we broke-up. Moreover, I also found out from her classmates that she was already cheated on me while we were still into the relationship. And that convinced me to moved forward and moved on to my life without her.

The Five (5) Steps of Moving On

So, if you are wondering why I need to share my stories about my past relationships? Well, this is just to show you how I came up with the steps in moving on from break-ups. Furthermore, if these steps will be applied, a person can move on easily without some bitterness on his/her hearts.

Step 1

Cry Hard Enough

Yes, you've read it correctly. The first thing that you need to do after a break-up is to cry out loud. Some people see crying is a sign of weakness but the truth is, only strong people dare to cry if they are in pain. Some of them are just denials and decides not to cry. Instead, they are trying to find something else to focus on. Yes, part of the steps is focusing something else however, without releasing your pain, frustration, and hate will not put you anywhere. So, that's why you need to cry to release the pain that you have during or after the break-ups.

By crying, it gives a lot of benefits not just emotionally but also physically. In an emotional aspect, first, it gives you a soothing effect like calming yourself and reducing your distress. Second, it helps you to reduce pain and promote a sense of well-being. Lastly, it will enhance your mood and relieves your stress. On the other hand, in physical benefits, it will help you to fall asleep easily, help you fight bacteria by cleaning your eyes as tears contain a fluid called lysozyme and improve your visions by keeping your eyes moist and preventing mucous membranes from drying out.

You know, whether you are a man or a woman, expressing true emotions will give you an uplifting feeling. Feelings are one of God's given abilities to us humans and we must utilize it in our own benefits. So, as what I've said, cry out loud or cry out in silence even how many days and nights it takes, do it and don't hold your feelings. Release it as much as you can however, when you finish your sobbing, grieving and crying, make a promise to yourself not to cry again for the same reason/s. Said to yourself "Enough is enough" and that's the clue that you are ready for the next step.

The Five (5) Steps of Moving On

But take note, don't proceed to the next step if you don't decide it yet to get over from your grief and if you don't know how to stop yourself from crying every time you think of him/her.

In moving on there are no shortcuts, that's why I wrote this book for everyone who will need it. Because if you take the shortcuts, you may end up in the same situation as your relations before. You may end up getting hurt because you did not try to internalize the lessons that you need to learn from your previous relationship.

So, don't take the shortcuts in moving on because if you wanted to, even if it takes months, you will get there.

Step 2

Accept What Happened!

The second step of moving on after spending your time grieving someone even though he/she is not dead yet is called acceptance. Acceptance means even if you think about him/her, you still do feel the pain but you choose to agree to take what happened to your relationship. I'm not saying here about denials of your feelings, you still need to acknowledge that you've been hurt so that you will know how to handle it.

You need to accept that he/she is not part of your life anymore. That you need to go to other chapters of your life without the one that you love. Yet, maybe you will be asking me how to accept that the one you love was no longer with you? Well, it takes time and effort and I will reveal here the technique that I'd learned from the Philippine movie "The Day After Valentines".

You know, it is very ironic because sometimes when you are in a relationship, from time to time you almost noticed all the bad sides and attitudes of that person and occasionally complained about it. However, when you broke-up, all you can think about that person was all his/her good qualities. You always remember all the best things that you've shared together. You always recalled all the memories of how happy you are together.

Thus, our technique is very simple. This is from the Philippine movie "The Day After Valentines" which I personally used it in my broke-up experience. Once you recalled or think about him/her, think only the bad sides and qualities of that person. Write down the bad sides and qualities about that person every day until you will notice that every time you think about him/her, you will not feel so much pain in your heart compared before. Sometimes, you will just laugh thinking how silly you are grieving someone who was not deserved you.

 This exercise is good if you have someone like your parents, brother or sister and even your best friend that will keep track of your list of bad sides and qualities of that person and evaluate your situations or feelings towards your ex-boyfriend/girlfriend.

Take note, when you are in the process of acceptance, please detached yourself from the things that will keep you reminded of him/her. Delete all your contacts or any communications from him/her like cellphone number/s and social media. If you cannot delete or block him/her on social media, try to deactivate your account and reactivate it when you are fully moved on and better.

I know it will not be easy however as long as you can bear the pain when you think about him/her. Meaning, you already accepted he/she no longer with you to the next chapter of your life. So, when this comes, it means you are ready to proceed to the next step.

Step 3

Find Self-Love and Self-Worth

The third step is finding your Self-Love and Self-Worth. You must know that you are worthy enough to be happy again and to be love and in love again.

You know, sometimes during in a relationship period, you will forget your self-worth because you always prioritize him/her, or you always prioritize your relationship even it was already been a toxic relationship.

In this step, you must learn again how to have self-worth and self-love. You must love yourself first before loving someone else. You cannot give love if you don't have that in yourself first. In this step, sometimes people misunderstood because they feel that they already accepted their situation, so, they engage in other relationships again and without any particular reasons, what happened to the previous relationship, will definitely happen again. It is like history repeats itself. Mistakes will always come to those people who did not learn from it.

Therefore, don't get into a relationship again if you didn't really move on from your past. Because as what I've said, you will suffer and at the same time your new partner will also suffer or bear the burden of that relationship.

That's why you need to fix yourself first by finding your self-love and self-worth. By doing this, you will realize how important your life and others lives.

So, I need you to be true to yourself, if you really find that self-love, self-respect and self-worth, you are ready for the next step of this guide.

But if you are asking me, how can I find that self-worth and self-love? Well, I cannot directly answer that because every person has a different meaning of self-love and self-worth. It is for you to find out. All I can I say is, try to dig deep to yourself, have a self-reflection and self-evaluation.

Step 4

Personal Development

As a person, we must have continuous development for ourselves.

This is the next step if you find your self-worth, self-respect, and self-love. Because when you found those things or characteristics in yourself, you will be eager to improve yourself.

Personal development may differ from person to person, you may want to improve your physical or be had a healthy body, you may want to expand your attitudes toward life, you may want to get to the next level of your career, you may want to enhance your spiritual aspect or you just want to develop anything you wanted to improve yourself to a better person than before.

As life coaches always said, if you want to have a better love relationship, it also requires a better person of yourself. Be a better person compared to what you are before. Be an independent man or woman, so that when you are going into a relationship again, that person will be just a bonus to your life.

In my part, I focus my improvement on my career and financial area of my life. Why I choose that area of my life? Well, that's the area of my life where my ex-girlfriend was looking for. I don't have enough in that area even though I was the one paid all her tuition fees, allowances, and other expenses. I still lacked the finances that we needed to start our dream house and any material things that she wanted.

Thus, maybe in your part, look at all the areas in your life that are lacking like a physical or healthy body, career, finances, and attitudes. There might be different aspects in your life that you need to improve aside from what I've mentioned. No matter what it is, do it and get motivated to improve yourself for your own good, not for someone else.

Furthermore, by committing yourself to improve or be better, you will be focused on yourself more and eventually, you will not think the sad experienced. Moreover, by becoming a better version of yourself, you will attract also another better person in your life, in terms of friends, colleagues, or maybe the next partner of your life.

Always remember this, whether you are trying to move on from your relationship broke-up or not, always try to improve yourself from what you already are because that's the true nature of being human. Continuous Improvement.

Step 5

Ask Guidance and Be Thankful

to the Higher Power

This is the last step but not the least. You need to ask guidance to the Higher Power whether from GOD, ALLAH, SHIVAH, BUDDAH, the UNIVERSE or whatever religion you believe in. Ask guidance from Him so that, you will be guided on whatever path you will take.

I believed, we are here in this world guided by the Higher Power and only we can do is to ask and be prepared to receive what we've asked for.

So, I put this to be the last step because whatever you step you took before this last step, all of that will be useless if there's no Higher Power intervention on whatever you do and plan. So, be thankful to Him or the Universe that whatever happened in the past, you'd conquered it all and you became a better person with a greater purpose in life.

Moreover, ask guidance that whatever decisions that you will make in the future, it will bring joy and happiness to your heart and all the people surround you. And if ever you will make mistakes, since you are only human, ask Him or the Universe to be strong enough to accept and learn lessons from those mistakes.

So, that's all I can give you about this last step. Be thankful to the Higher Power and ask Him or the Universe for guidance in your life.

Conclusions

Given the Five (5) steps of moving on. Here are the steps. First, cry, sob or grief about what happened to your relationship because we are only humans, we will feel pain, frustrations, and sadness. So, it is okay to release all that pain in your heart. Second, accept that he/she no longer with you and you must move on to the next chapter of your life. Third, find your self-love and self-worth, because sometimes when we fall in love, we give all our love to our partner or to our relationship and the time that we no longer together with them, we forgot how to love ourselves again. Find a way how to love yourself again so that the love that you longing for will be already there and you will not be trying to find it in other people's love. Fourth, after you found your self-love and self-worth, it is time for your personal growth and development. By pursuing yourself to become a better person, you will love yourself more and you will feel that you are already been completed. And loving by someone else will be just a plus to your life. Last but not the least, be thankful to the Higher Power and ask Him or the Universe for guidance to your life.

This is the most comprehensive book for moving on from the break-ups. Internalize and execute the steps properly given in this book. Eventually, you will make your move on so easily. Moreover, you will be a better person and you will be a loving person compared yourself before.

I am hoping the steps in this book will be helpful because it helps me a lot based on my personal experienced. I found these steps more effective and easier to do because I'm changing my attitudes, my mindsets and myself. And that's the only factor that we have a control compared to trying to change the circumstances and to change someone else.

The Five (5) Steps of Moving On

Namaste, Goodluck, and God bless you. Always remember this. Love yourself and you deserve more and you are worthy enough to be who you are. Don't lose yourself trying to love someone else.

"And above all these put on love, which binds everything together in perfect harmony – Colossians 3:14"

The Five (5) Steps of Moving On

The Five (5) Steps of Moving On

The Five (5) Steps of Moving On

The Five (5) Steps of Moving On

The Five (5) Steps of Moving On

The Five (5) Steps of Moving On

www.ingramcontent.com/pod-product-compliance
Lightning Source LLC
Chambersburg PA
CBHW051145250726
48655CB00007B/3254